On the Front Line

FIGHTING THE VIETNAM WAR

Brian Fitzgerald

www.raintreepublishers.co.uk
Visit our website to find out more information about **Raintree** books.

To order:
☎ Phone 44 (0) 1865 888113
📄 Send a fax to 44 (0) 1865 314091
💻 Visit the Raintree Bookshop at **www.raintreepublishers.co.uk** to browse our catalogue and order online.

Produced for Raintree by
White-Thomson Publishing Ltd,
Bridgewater Business Centre,
210 High Street, Lewes, BN7 2NH

First published in Great Britain by Raintree,
Halley Court, Jordan Hill, Oxford OX2 8EJ,
part of Harcourt Education.
Raintree is a registered trademark of
Harcourt Education Ltd.

© Harcourt Education Ltd 2005.
The moral right of the proprietor has been asserted.

Editorial: Juliet Smith and Daniel Nunn
Design: Michelle Lisseter
Picture Research: Amy Sparks
Project Manager: Juliet Smith
Production: Duncan Gilbert

Originated by Dot Gradations Ltd
Printed and bound in China by South China
Printing Company Ltd

ISBN 1 844 43690 X
09 08 07 06 05
10 9 8 7 6 5 4 3 2 1

**British Library Cataloguing in
Publication Data**
Fitzgerald, Brian
Fighting the Vietnam War. – (On the Front Line)
1. Vietnamese Conflict, 1961-1975 – Juvenile literature
I. Title
959.7'043
A full catalogue record for this book is
available from the British Library.

Acknowledgements
The publishers would like to thank the following for
permission to reproduce photographs and maps:
Art Archive pp. **17**, **27**; AKG p. **22**; Alamy p. **32**;
Camerapress p. **9**; Corbis pp. **7**, **8**, **10**, **12**, **13**, **14**,
16(l), **20**, **23**, **24**(l), **25**(r), **28**, **29**, **30**, **31**, **34–35**, **36**,
39, **41**; Harcourt p. **26**; Popperfoto pp. **34**(l), **35**(r), **38**;
Topfoto pp. **4–5**, **6**, **11**, **15**, **16**(r), **18**, **19**, **21**(l), **21**(r),
22(l), **24–25**, **33**, **37**, **40**. Cover photograph shows US
troops loaded with equipment setting out on a patrol,
reproduced with permission of AKG.

Map on p. 6 by Peter Bull.

Source notes: pp. **26–27** *The Tunnels of Cu Chi: The
Untold Story of Vietnam* by Tom Mangold and John
Penycate; pp. **28–29** Quote from Nguyen Cong Hoan
taken from *Vietnam: A Portrait of its People at War* by
David Chanoff and Doan Van Toai; pp. **34–35** Quote
from Do Ba taken from a Thanh Nien newspaper article
dated 16 March 1998; pp. **36–37** Quote from Nguyen
Thi Duc taken from the documentary series *Vietnam: A
Television History*; pp. **38–39** Quote from Colonel Bui Tin
taken from the documentary series *Vietnam: A Television
History*.

Every effort has been made to contact copyright holders
of any material reproduced in this book. Any omissions
will be rectified in subsequent printings if notice is given
to the publishers.

The paper used to print this book comes from
sustainable resources.

CONTENTS

Any words appearing in the text in bold, **like this**, are explained in the glossary. You can also look out for them in the Word Bank box at the bottom of each page.

A STRANGE NEW WORLD

International conflict

During the Vietnam War, the South Vietnamese fought against **Communist** troops from North Vietnam. The South Vietnamese were supported by troops from the United States, Australia, South Korea, New Zealand, the Philippines, and Thailand. Many questions about why the war was fought are still to be answered.

A US marine sergeant wades through a stream deep in the jungle of the Mekong Delta in Vietnam. He and the other ten members of his squad are exhausted. They have been on **patrol** for four days. Each man carries 27 kilograms (60 pounds) of equipment through streams and jungles. The sound of machine gun fire is never far away. The sergeant knows he has to stay alert. Viet Cong **rebels** could surprise his squad at any moment. One false move might set off a **booby trap** that could kill him or one of his men. This is not the type of war he had expected. The battlefields are jungles and small villages.

US soldiers needed to stay alert during their patrols in Vietnam. Rivers and streams might contain hidden traps.

Word Bank   allies   countries that are on the same side during a war
patrol   search for enemy troops

The sergeant just needs to stay alive for two more months before his **tour of duty** will end and he can go home. His home seems like it is a million miles away. He is only twenty years old.

A new enemy

Only a few years earlier, most Americans could not find Vietnam on a map. During World War II the Vietnamese had helped the United States defeat Japan. Now the former **allies** were at war. Like so many others, including millions of people back home, the soldier wonders, "How did we get here?"

Find out later

What is Agent Orange?

What is a POW?

Who were the tunnel rats?

rebel person who fights against the people who are in power
tour of duty period of time spent in active military service

THE FIRST WAR

Ho Chi Minh

Ho Chi Minh became a supporter of Communism while living in France. He brought his Communist beliefs back to his homeland and there he led the fight for Vietnam's independence until his death in 1969. His name means "he who **enlightens**".

In the 1880s, France took control of the Asian countries of Vietnam, Laos, and Cambodia and named their new **colony** French Indochina. France grew rich from Vietnam's natural resources, but most Vietnamese people stayed poor. During World War II, the Japanese defeated the French in Vietnam. A **Communist** called Ho Chi Minh organized an army to free his homeland. Ho's army, called the Vietminh, used US weapons to fight the Japanese invaders. When Japan surrendered to the United States on 2 September 1945, Ho Chi Minh declared Vietnam a free nation.

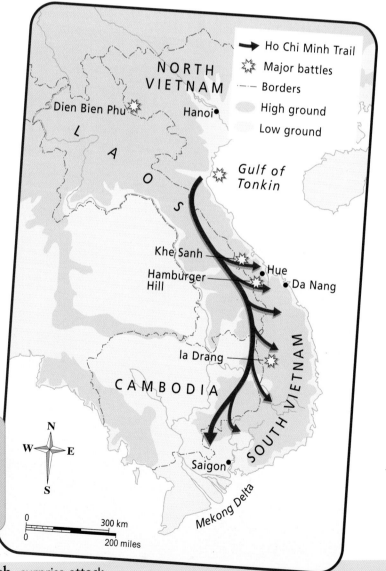

A map of Vietnam showing the Ho Chi Minh Trail, and the sites of some of the key battles of the Vietnam War.

Word Bank ambush surprise attack
artillery large mounted guns that fire shells or missiles

Fighting the French

A few weeks later, French troops returned to take back Vietnam. The Vietminh did not have the weapons to fight a normal battle. Instead they used **guerrilla** warfare. The Vietminh attacked French troops in hit-and-run **ambushes**, often at night. Over the next nine years, these tactics wore down the French troops' desire to fight.

In 1954, the French tried to force the Vietminh into a face-to-face battle in a valley in northern Vietnam called Dien Bien Phu. The Vietminh surprised the 16,500 French troops with an army of 50,000 soldiers. They pounded the French base with heavy **artillery** and quickly surrounded them. The French soldiers held out for 56 days before they finally surrendered on 7 May 1954. During the battle, 2200 French soldiers and 8000 Vietminh were killed.

Digging tunnels

An important weapon for the Vietminh at Dien Bien Phu was the shovel! They used shovels to dig tunnels and trenches that allowed them to surround the French troops and cut off their **supply lines**.

Vietnamese troops charge up a hill during the battle for Dien Bien Phu.

colony   country that is ruled by another, more powerful, country
guerrilla   soldier who is not part of a regular army

Mini timeline:

7 May 1954 – French surrender at Dien Bien Phu.

21 July 1954 – Vietnam is divided in half at a peace conference in Geneva, Switzerland.

March 1959 – Ho Chi Minh declares a "people's war" to unite the divided country.

November 1960 – John F. Kennedy elected US president.

April 1961 – Kennedy sends the first US Special Forces to South Vietnam.

July 1962 – Australia sends its first army advisers to South Vietnam.

A divided country

The fighting between the Vietminh and the French occurred during the height of the **Cold War** between the **Soviet Union** and the United States. During their fight against the French, Ho Chi Minh's troops had received weapons and money from the Soviet Union and China. The United States did not want the **Communists** to gain power in Vietnam, so it spent more than a billion dollars to support the French.

After the defeat at Dien Bien Phu, France took its troops out of Vietnam. But Ho Chi Minh did not gain control of the whole country. A peace agreement split Vietnam into two parts. The Communists controlled North Vietnam.

A US military adviser trains South Vietnamese troops.
➡

Word Bank   Cold War   rivalry between the Soviet Union and the United States that began after World War II and lasted until the 1990s

The leaders of South Vietnam opposed Communism and gained the support of the United States. The land between the two areas was called the Demilitarized Zone, or DMZ.

The South under attack

Ho Chi Minh and the Communists wanted to control all of Vietnam. Communist **rebels** called the Viet Cong tried to gain power in the South. Most of the South Vietnamese army, called the Army of the Republic of Vietnam (ARVN), did not have the training or **combat** experience of the Viet Cong. The United States sent money, weapons, and military advisers to South Vietnam. However, the US President John F. Kennedy believed his country needed to do more. He increased the number of US **Special Forces** soldiers in South Vietnam.

Ho Chi Minh Trail

The North Vietnamese moved weapons and supplies to the Viet Cong in South Vietnam along the Ho Chi Minh Trail (see page 6). Most people either walked or rode bicycles (see photo on the left). It could take as long as six months to move supplies down the Trail.

combat fighting
Special Forces top soldiers in the US army

THE UNITED STATES STEPS IN

Ap Bac

The battle of Ap Bac in South Vietnam was an early signal that the Viet Cong were a powerful enemy. On 2 January 1963, 350 Viet Cong soldiers defeated a South Vietnamese force that was four times larger and had better weapons.

United States **Special Forces** in South Vietnam were supposed to be there to teach the South Vietnamese army and native people how to use **guerrilla** warfare against the Viet Cong. But sometimes Special Forces troops found themselves in the middle of the fighting.

Battle at Nam Dang

On 6 June 1964, for example, the Viet Cong attacked a Special Forces camp at Nam Dong in South Vietnam. Captain Roger Donlon led the defence of the camp. He dodged heavy enemy gunfire and **grenades** as he rushed to close the main gate. There, he killed three Viet Cong soldiers who planned to blow up the gate. Donlon was shot in the stomach, but he kept fighting.

South Vietnamese soldiers guard two captured Viet Cong guerrillas while a US soldier looks on.

Word Bank   ammunition   bullets that are fired from a weapon
Medal of Honour   top medal awarded by the US army

Donlon then ran to a **mortar** position where he found some of his men who had also been hit. He fired at the enemy and gave the injured men time to pull back. Donlon was hit by an enemy mortar round in the shoulder but he found the strength to move his mortar to a new position. There he found three more injured men.

Bravery awarded

Donlon was hit a third time as he dragged **ammunition** to his men, but still he did not stop fighting. Donlon's courage helped to inspire his men to victory. They finally defeated the Viet Cong at Nam Dong and Donlon became the first US soldier in Vietnam to earn a Medal of Honour from the US army. He is still alive today.

Agent Orange

In 1962, US planes began spraying the chemical Agent Orange over South Vietnamese jungles, killing many thousands of trees (see photograph below). The United States hoped this would make it easier to spot the Viet Cong. Agent Orange was later found to cause cancer and birth defects.

mortar small, portable cannon

US President Johnson wanted to end the war quickly without losing too many US soldiers. He sent US warplanes to bomb the Ho Chi Minh Trail and other key targets in North Vietnam. This operation was called Rolling Thunder.

New president, new strategy

On 22 November 1963, President Kennedy was **assassinated**. Lyndon Johnson took over as president of the United States. Johnson was worried about Vietnam. The Viet Cong were growing stronger in South Vietnam. Johnson wanted to send more troops, but he knew most Americans would not support that.

Attack in the Gulf of Tonkin

On 2 August 1964, the USS *Maddox* was sailing off the Vietnamese coast in the Gulf of Tonkin. Three North Vietnamese **patrol** boats appeared and began heading towards the **destroyer**. The commander of the *Maddox*, Herbert L. Ogier, ordered his crew to fire three warning shots. When the patrol boats ignored the warning, the *Maddox* opened fire.

President Johnson (second from right) met with his advisers on 4 August 1964 to discuss the crisis in the Gulf of Tonkin.

Word Bank   assassinated murdered
destroyer fast, lightly armoured but heavily armed warship

The *Maddox* scored one direct hit and damaged a second boat. The *Maddox* also avoided two **torpedoes** launched by one of the boats. Two days after leaving the Gulf, the *Maddox* and another destroyer named *Turner Joy* returned. The crews of both ships reported being attacked. The United States then sent F-8 jet planes to attack North Vietnamese patrol boats in the area.

The President gains power

President Johnson believed the attacks showed that the North Vietnamese wanted to start a war with the United States and much of the American public now agreed with him. He asked the US Congress to approve the Gulf of Tonkin **Resolution**. This gave the President the power to use any means he needed to stop further attacks.

What happened?

There is no real proof that the second attack, involving the *Maddox* and *Turner Joy* (see photograph below), really happened. The North Vietnamese deny firing at the US ships. US crews claimed that they hit at least three enemy boats, but no wreckage or bodies were ever found.

resolution   formal decision that is agreed upon by a vote
torpedo   missile that is fired under water

DANGER IN THE AIR

Thunder rolls on

Operation Rolling Thunder was supposed to last a few months, but it went on for more than three years. Thousands of Vietnamese were killed. Many bridges, roads, and buildings were hit, but were soon repaired. The Ho Chi Minh Trail also stayed open. The **campaign** had failed.

Captain Merlyn Dethlefsen climbed into his F-105 Thunderchief plane. He was about to take off on a Rolling Thunder bombing mission deep in North Vietnam. His target was a **surface-to-air missile (SAM)** site that protected an important steel factory. His mission was to destroy the SAMs so other US bombers could destroy the steel works without being fired at.

Things did not go as planned, however. The SAM site was surrounded by **artillery**. The sky was filled with black clouds from enemy gunfire. Dethlefsen flew towards the ground to avoid missiles from attacking **MiG** jet fighters. His plane was badly damaged by a shell from an enemy cannon.

Word Bank   campaign   series of related missions that form a phase of a war

Mission complete

Dethlefsen could have headed for safety, but refused. He knew the bombers would not stand a chance against the SAMs. The lives of the US crews depended on him. Dethlefsen made five passes over the steel works. He dodged fire from 96 enemy cannon on the ground and four **MiG** fighters in the air. The brave captain destroyed two SAM sites.

Just doing his job

Dethlefsen's bravery allowed the bomber pilots to wipe out their targets without losing any planes. "All I did was the job I was sent to do," Dethlefsen later said. He had bravely completed his mission and safely made it back to his base. Many other US pilots would not be so lucky.

Napalm

US planes did not just drop bombs. Many also dropped **napalm**. This sticky gel made from gasoline burst into flames when it hit the air. Napalm was meant to destroy military targets, but it also burned thousands of **civilians**. The child in the photograph above was badly burned in a napalm strike.

A flight of three F-105s refuel in the air on their way to bombing targets in North Vietnam in 1966.
◄

Shot down over Hanoi

In October 1967, US Navy pilot John McCain took off on a bombing raid. His target was Hanoi, the capital of North Vietnam. He did not return for more than five years. An enemy missile blew off his plane's right wing. McCain ejected from his plane. The force broke his right knee and both his arms.

McCain landed in a lake and almost drowned. An angry mob pulled him to shore. Troops soon arrived to take him away. McCain was taken to a prison that US pilots called the Hanoi Hilton. He was a **prisoner of war** (POW).

Brutal treatment

John McCain wrote about his terrible experiences as a prisoner in a book called *Faith of My Fathers*. Here he remembers being beaten:

"Shouting and laughing, they bashed me around the room, slamming their fists into my face and body, kicking and stomping me when I fell."

These captured US pilots were forced to march through the streets of Hanoi.

John McCain (bottom right) poses with other US Navy pilots in 1965. He later became a US senator.

Word Bank missing in action term used to describe a soldier who does not return from a war alive and whose body is never found

Prisoner of war

McCain lay in an empty cell for four days before his captors took him to hospital. A doctor put one of McCain's arms in a cast. He did not fix the other arm. McCain did not receive an operation on his knee for more than a month.

The North Vietnamese tried to force him to tell them military secrets. McCain refused. The guards put him in his own cell. He was not allowed to see or talk to other prisoners for two years. Later, they planned to release McCain, but he refused to leave his fellow prisoners behind. The guards made him pay by **torturing** him for four days. He was not released until March 1973.

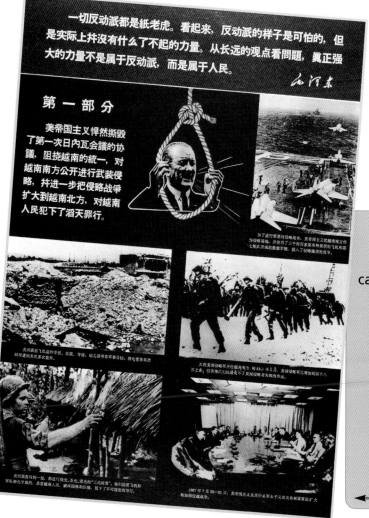

POWs and MIAs

- 802 prisoners were released by North Vietnam at the end of the war

- 661 of these were US military men. Nearly 500 were pilots who had been shot down.

- 141 were **civilians**

- 36 prisoners escaped during the war

- 2583 US military personnel were listed as **missing in action (MIA)**.

This North Vietnamese poster calls the United States "paper tiger". This meant that it was not as powerful as it seemed. The **Communists** used anti-United States posters like this one to try to win new supporters in South Vietnam.

torture beatings and pain inflicted on prisoners, often to get secret information out of them

LOOKING FOR A HIDDEN ENEMY

On 8 March 1965, the first US ground troops arrived in Vietnam. Their job was to protect the base at Da Nang, so planes could safely carry out bombing missions in North Vietnam.

The draft

The United States' new plan in Vietnam needed many more troops. The US government began to **draft** young men between the ages of 18 and 25 for military service. More than two million American men were drafted between 1965 and 1972.

The search begins

The original mission of the US troops had been to defend key positions in the south. However, soldiers from the North Vietnamese army now supported the Viet Cong. The South Vietnamese army alone could not stop its enemies from gaining control of the towns and villages in South Vietnam. The United States decided to adopt a new strategy called "search and destroy". US troops would hunt down their enemy and wipe it out. By the end of the year, more than 180,000 US troops had arrived in Vietnam.

US soldiers sometimes burned down Vietnamese villages during "search and destroy" missions because they suspected the villagers were helping the Viet Cong.

Word Bank   covert secret
draft order someone into military service

Early clashes

US troops faced the North Vietnamese army for the first time in the Battle of Ia Drang, which was at its fiercest from 14 to 17 November 1965. The North Vietnamese army had more men, but the US troops had air support from **gunships** and bombers. The North Vietnamese army suffered more than 2500 casualties and was pushed out of the area.

The North Vietnamese lost the battle, but they learned an important lesson. They did not have the firepower to match the United States. For the rest of the war they would use the same **guerrilla** tactics that had helped them defeat the French. They would try to break the Americans' will to keep fighting.

Help from "down under"

The United States was not the only country to send troops to support South Vietnam. South Korea sent more than 300,000 troops and Australia sent about 50,000 men. Members of the Australian Special Air Service sometimes teamed up with US Green Berets for **covert** missions.

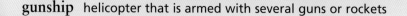

An Australian soldier wearing a jungle "boonie" hat takes cover behind a tree.

---

gunship   helicopter that is armed with several guns or rockets

Help from above

Helicopters played a huge role in Vietnam. Soldiers called them "Hueys" or choppers. Choppers were used to transport troops in and out of **hostile** territory. They often needed to fly very close to enemy fire. The men who flew choppers were extremely brave.

On 14 November, during the Battle of Ia Drang, a **battalion** of US soldiers was surrounded by North Vietnamese troops. The Americans were running low on **ammunition**. Their commander would not let any helicopters land because it was too dangerous. One pilot knew the men needed help, so he decided to land anyway.

Search and rescue

Helicopters saved many lives in Vietnam. Each day they landed in dangerous **combat** areas and took wounded soldiers to hospitals. Helicopters rescued more than 500,000 injured soldiers. Many chopper crews were killed or wounded trying to rescue their **comrades**.

US troops jump from a Huey into battle. The helicopter played an important role in the Vietnam War.

Word Bank   battalion   large military unit made up of 300 to 1000 troops
comrade   fellow soldier

A heroic pilot

Captain Ed Freeman flew through heavy gunfire to deliver ammunition, water, and medical supplies to the soldiers on the ground. He made the trip many times, even though his helicopter was not armed with any weapons. Without his bravery, many more troops might have been killed.

Many of the soldiers on the ground were injured. Medical choppers refused to fly into the area. They did not want to risk getting shot down. Freeman knew the men might die without medical care. He and his crew flew fourteen separate missions to **evacuate** the injured. They rescued more than 30 wounded men. Freeman lived to tell his incredible story of bravery. He retired from the US army in 1967.

Mail call

Choppers brought many supplies to soldiers. Some soldiers say the most important delivery was the mail. Soldiers in Vietnam had no other contact with family or friends. A letter from home could help them forget about the horrors of war.

An injured US marine is carried to a helicopter.

Trouble in the jungle

The search and destroy missions led US troops into the jungles of Vietnam. Small squads of about a dozen men moved through the mud and **rice paddies**. These foot soldiers were nicknamed "grunts".

Each man carried all his equipment on his back. These packs could weigh as much as 32 kilograms (70 pounds). Soldiers and their equipment often got tangled in vines. They called these "wait a minute vines" because one grunt had to tell the rest of his squad to "wait a minute" while he tried to remove the vines. Vietnam has a tropical **climate**. This meant that grunts in the jungle were usually wet and cold during the **monsoon season** and hot and sweaty in the summer.

trap

- Toe popper – bullet placed on a sharp bamboo stake that would fire when stepped on.
- Punji stakes – sharp bamboo stakes placed in a small hole and covered with leaves (see photograph below).

US troops loaded with gear set out on a patrol.

Word Bank   climate   weather conditions for a certain area
monsoon season   period of wind and rain in southern Asia

Grunts also had to be careful not to set off **booby traps**. **Tripwires** tied between trees on land or in streams could set off hidden bombs.

Invisible enemy

The Viet Cong liked to hide in the thick jungle. They **ambushed** US troops without any warning. Grunts did not get much sleep because they knew the Viet Cong often attacked at night. Soldiers grew frustrated because they often could not see their enemy. There was no way to tell an innocent farmer from an enemy soldier. The frequent **guerrilla** attacks by the Viet Cong took many lives and also damaged **morale**.

Chow time

Soldiers on **patrol** usually ate **combat rations** (C-rations). A C-ration box might contain a can of hot dogs and beans, peaches, and a piece of cake. The box would also include salt, pepper, sugar, chewing gum, toilet paper, and cigarettes.

A grunt takes a break from patrol to eat his C-rations.

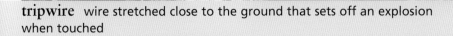

tripwire wire stretched close to the ground that sets off an explosion when touched

23

R and R

Soldiers who returned from patrols were sometimes given a few days of rest and relaxation (called "R and R"). Many soldiers went to Saigon, the South Vietnamese capital. Others went to camps that had beautiful beaches where they could swim and sunbathe, as shown in the photograph below.

Trouble in the water

Small US Navy boats called swift boats **patrolled** the Mekong Delta in South Vietnam. The Americans did not want the Viet Cong to use the river as a **supply line**. They also wanted to capture or kill the many Viet Cong soldiers who hid along the waterway.

John Kerry was in charge of a swift boat and its five-man crew. One night, on 19 March 1969, Kerry was told that another boat had come under attack. Kerry and his crew rushed to help. A Viet Cong rocket exploded near his boat. Kerry ordered his crew to beach the boat on the shore. He jumped off the boat.

On the beach, Kerry saw a Viet Cong soldier with a rocket launcher. One rocket could destroy the boat and kill his crew. Kerry killed the Viet Cong soldier before he could fire at the boat.

Swift action

On 28 March 1969, Kerry's boat came under fire again. A mine blew up near his boat. Kerry's arm was injured when a second mine **detonated**. Kerry discovered that one of his men had fallen overboard. Enemy **snipers** were firing at the man in the water. Kerry knew he had to save his fellow soldier. He ordered his crew to fire at the enemy. Kerry's arm was bleeding and he was in pain, but he still reached into the water and pulled the man on to his boat.

Purple Hearts

John Kerry received three Purple Heart medals for his actions in Vietnam. When he returned to the United States he became a vocal **protester** against the war and later became a US senator. In 2004 he ran for president of the United States, but was beaten by George W. Bush.

Three US patrol boats cruise the Mekong River in search of Viet Cong **guerrillas**.

MEET THE PRESS

JOHN KERRY
"Vietnam Veterans Against the War"

In April 1971, John Kerry (right) appeared on a popular US television news programme called *Meet the Press* to speak out against the Vietnam War.

sniper hidden soldier who shoots enemy soldiers from long distances with a special gun

The underground world

The Viet Cong also faced many dangers. They built a series of tunnels in South Vietnam to hide from US troops and take cover from bombs. They did not have many resources so they had to come up with some very clever ways to survive.

Hospital under fire

Viet Cong doctor Vo Hoang Le had been operating on patients for three days. Le did not work in an ordinary hospital. It was located 5 metres (15 feet) under ground! Some of the instruments he used were made from parts of shot-down US planes and helicopters.

American troops were moving towards the tunnel that led to the hospital. Le's medical staff wanted to retreat.

The Viet Cong used underground cities such as this one to hide from US attacks.

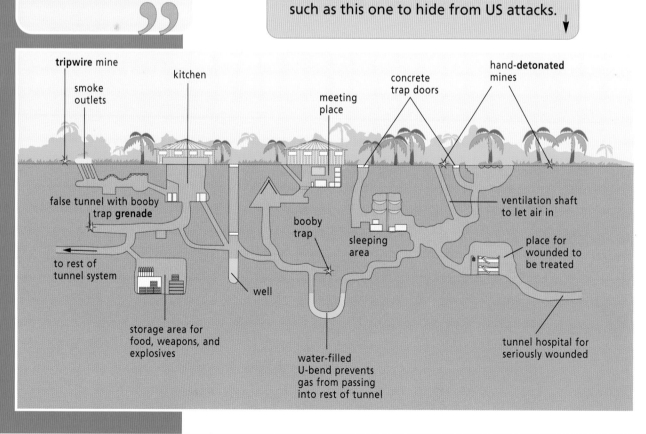

tripwire mine

smoke outlets

kitchen

meeting place

concrete trap doors

hand-**detonated** mines

false tunnel with booby trap **grenade**

booby trap

ventilation shaft to let air in

to rest of tunnel system

sleeping area

place for wounded to be treated

well

storage area for food, weapons, and explosives

water-filled U-bend prevents gas from passing into rest of tunnel

tunnel hospital for seriously wounded

Word Bank   spider hole   small one-person hole that is covered with leaves

However, Le could not let his 60 wounded patients be captured. He hid in a **spider hole** and waited. Eventually, Le saw three US soldiers moving towards him. Very frightened, but determined, he fired his gun. All three soldiers fell to the ground. The doctor had become a soldier.

Amazing courage

A few months later, Le was defending another hospital when he was shot in the right hand. He was bleeding badly and his little finger was hanging by a piece of skin. Le tore his finger off and bandaged his hand. He could no longer use his right hand, so he taught himself how to perform **surgery** left-handed.

Oh rats!

The brave US soldiers who explored Viet Cong tunnels were known as tunnel rats. They carried a pistol, a knife, and a torch into the dark, narrow tunnels. There they faced many dangers including **booby traps**, snakes, and being shot at by Viet Cong soldiers.

This soldier is being lowered into a tunnel as part of a search and destroy mission.

surgery medical operation

THE TIDE TURNS

Surprise attack

The Tet Offensive also surprised South Vietnamese **civilians**. Nguyen Cong Hoan remembers the terror of the surprise attack:

"It began around midnight with what everyone first thought were firecrackers. When we realized a battle was going on we rushed out of the house and ran toward the beach. Thousands of people were on the beach watching the explosions and the planes swooping down and the great balls of orange fire."

In January 1968, both sides agreed to stop fighting so that Vietnamese soldiers on both sides could celebrate their new year, called "Tet". Many South Vietnamese troops went home to their families. On 30 January, Viet Cong and North Vietnamese troops broke the **truce.** More than 80,000 troops launched a surprise assault on more than 100 South Vietnamese cities in the attack known as the Tet Offensive.

The Tet Offensive

Many of the troops focused on taking key buildings in Saigon, the capital of South Vietnam. Viet Cong **guerrillas** broke into the grounds of the US **embassy** and killed four Americans. The embassy was not made safe until several hours later. Despite the initial losses, however, the US military quickly recovered from the surprise attack. They took back most of the country in only a few days.

US troops attempt to secure the streets of Saigon after the Tet Offensive of 1968.

Word Bank   embassy   government building of one country that is located in a foreign country

In the ancient city of Hue, a bloody battle raged for nearly a month. US troops fought through the streets to regain control of the city. The **Communist**s were finally driven out. Most of Hue's buildings had been destroyed during the battle. More than 100,000 people became **refugees**.

A losing victory?

The Communists had hoped their attack would cause the South Vietnamese people to rise up against their government. They did not achieve their goal. The Communists lost ten times as many men as the United States and the South Vietnamese army. The Tet Offensive was a military victory for the United States, but it was a major defeat in other ways.

A long siege

About a week before Tet, the North Vietnamese attacked a US marine base at Khe Sanh. It was not a very important base, but the United States refused to let it fall. The siege of Khe Sanh lasted 77 days before North Vietnamese forces were driven out.

US marines fire a heavy machine gun at North Vietnamese troops during the battle of Khe Sanh.

refugees   people forced to leave their home, usually during a war
truce   agreement to stop fighting

A television war

The Vietnam War was called the first television war. The American public saw the horror of war each night on the evening news. They saw troops being killed and towns destroyed by bombing. Television news reports helped build a negative view of the war.

Trouble at home

At the beginning of 1968, many Americans believed the United States was close to winning the war. Since the fighting had started, US troops had not lost any major battles. After the Tet Offensive many people changed their minds. It seemed now that the **Communists** were still very powerful and that the United States could not win the war.

Protests

Major war protests had been taking place in the United States since 1965. Many Americans did not think their country should be fighting an enemy that was not a direct threat to the United States. As the war dragged on, Americans grew tired of sending their young men to die in Vietnam.

Images like this one of three wounded US soldiers were very common during the Vietnam War. They started to turn Americans against the war. ↓

Word Bank demonstrations group protests
draft cards official letters ordering a person to enter the military

The protests increased after the Tet Offensive. People from all walks of life joined **demonstrations** calling for an end to the war. Students on college campuses refused to go to lectures. Many young men burned their **draft cards**. Others went to Canada or Europe to avoid going to war. Even many **veterans** of the war joined in the protest movement.

New leader

In March 1968, President Johnson announced that he would not run for re-election. He was worn down by the war in Vietnam and the protests at home. Another president would have to find a way to end the war. In November 1968, Richard Nixon was elected US president.

Racism?

Many college students were excused from the **draft** until they finished college. But people with low incomes, many of whom were black, could not usually afford college. Many African Americans believed the draft was **racist** because it singled out people with less education, many of whom were black.

> War **protesters** block the entrance to the US Capitol building in Washington DC.

racist   someone who hates someone else because of the colour of their skin
veteran   person who served in the armed forces

A PROMISE OF PEACE

Before the election, President Nixon had promised to bring "peace with honour". He said he had a plan for ending the war, not winning it. He called it "Vietnamization". This meant that the South Vietnamese army would take over most of the fighting, using US weapons and being trained by US troops. Then the Americans would be able to go home.

Nixon's plan

Many things went wrong with the plan. The South Vietnamese army was in bad shape. Many officers were not good leaders. Soldiers did not have enough time to train and seemed afraid to fight. They were used to having US troops fight for them. Many South Vietnamese troops **deserted**.

Many US soldiers wanted peace in Vietnam just as much as the people back in the United States.

Word Bank   addict   person who cannot stop doing something or using something
deserted   left without permission

Soldiers want out

Nixon's plan hurt the **morale** of the US troops. Their goal had been to win the war. Now, they just wanted to get home alive. No one wanted to be the last soldier to die in Vietnam. They knew about the war protests back in the United States. Many soldiers were also against the war. Some refused to follow orders to fight. Others deserted their **platoons**.

Officers as targets

Many soldiers disliked their commanding officers. Some thought officers cared more about their own careers than the lives of their men. These troops "fragged" their commanders. This meant they tried to kill or injure the officers by throwing **grenades** or shooting at them. Nearly 800 cases of fragging were reported in Vietnam.

Battle for Hamburger Hill

The battle for Hamburger Hill, in May 1969, showed why many people were against the war. Seventy US soldiers died and 372 were wounded. But the army abandoned the hill shortly after taking it because they thought that they did not need it to win the battle. All the bloodshed had been for no good reason.

US troops rush a wounded **comrade** to a helicopter during the battle for Hamburger Hill.

heroin harmful, illegal drug
platoon small army unit usually made up of 16 to 44 men

"Frightened children

Do Ba was only eight years old at the time of the My Lai massacre. Here, he remembers the horrors of having to hide under dead bodies:

"I was small so I was buried among the dead bodies of others. My whole body was soaked with their blood."

More problems for Nixon

President Nixon had other problems to face back in the United States. In November 1969, the public learned of the horrible **massacre** of hundreds of Vietnamese **civilians**.

Revenge mission

More than a year earlier, a **platoon** of US soldiers had arrived in a small village called My Lai. The men had been told that many Viet Cong troops were in the area. The US troops wanted revenge for their friends who had been killed or injured by **booby traps** and **snipers**.

Vietnamese civilians often found themselves in the line of fire. Here, an elderly woman and her grandchild take cover in a field.

Word Bank   horrified   shocked
massacre   killing a large number of innocent people

The US troops found only women, children, and old men in the village. Not a single shot was fired at the US soldiers. But they still wanted revenge. They took out their anger on the helpless villagers. Over the next four hours, the US troops murdered as many as 500 innocent people. The troops slaughtered the very people they were supposed to be protecting.

Outrage

The My Lai massacre was kept secret for more than a year. Once the truth came out, Americans were **outraged** that their government had lied to them. They were even angrier that a small group of US troops could commit such an awful crime. Even Americans who supported the war were **horrified**.

Student deaths

On 4 May 1970, US National Guard troops were called in to break up a war protest at Kent State University in Ohio. The soldiers shot **tear gas** into the crowd of students, but the **protesters** still did not leave (see photograph below). Then they started shooting at the unarmed students. Four died and nine others were injured. The violence shocked the world and sparked hundreds more protests around the United States.

This elderly South Vietnamese man is being led away by a US soldier who suspects him of supporting the Viet Cong.

outraged   made very angry
tear gas   type of gas that makes your eyes fill with tears

Nguyen Thi Duc survived the Christmas bombings of Hanoi in December 1972, but many members of his family were not as lucky. He remembers:

"The shelter collapsed on me. The next morning, I was taken to the hospital. Only later did I learn that five members of my family had been killed."

Peace talks between the United States and the **Communists** from North Vietnam had begun in 1968. The talks dragged on for several years. Both sides wanted to end the war, but neither wanted to give up too much to its enemy. In October 1972, they finally agreed on a settlement.

No deal

The South Vietnamese did not like the terms of the settlement. They also knew their country would collapse without the help of the Americans so they refused to sign the deal. This angered the North Vietnamese. The peace talks ground to a halt. On 18 December 1972, President Nixon ordered a massive bombing raid on Hanoi. This became known as the Christmas bombings.

The Christmas bombings left much of Hanoi in ruins.

Word Bank   ceasefire an end to fighting

The Christmas bombings

Over twelve days, giant B-52 bombers dropped thousands of tons of bombs on Hanoi. It was the most intense bombing attack of the war. The North Vietnamese finally agreed to negotiate again. They did not want to see any more of their homeland destroyed.

A new agreement

The United States and North Vietnam reached a new deal. The South Vietnamese had no choice but to approve it. The last US **combat** troops left Vietnam on 29 March 1973. More than 58,000 Americans had been killed. More than 300,000 were wounded. Billions of dollars had been spent and nothing had been gained. The South Vietnamese were now left to fight alone.

Peace details

The 1973 peace agreement stated that:

- there would be a **ceasefire** in Vietnam

- armies on both sides would keep whatever land they currently held

- US troops would leave Vietnam within 60 days

- all **prisoners of war** would be returned.

A former US prisoner of war is reunited with his family in March 1973.

Renewed fighting

Both the North and South Vietnamese soon broke the peace agreement. The two sides once again fought to control the land in South Vietnam. The South Vietnamese were no longer protected by the experienced US troops. The South Vietnamese army was running out of supplies and **morale** was low.

The United States had promised to help South Vietnam if the **Communists** broke the peace agreement. But when the fighting broke out, the United States did not respond. US leaders were no longer interested in supporting this unpopular war.

One last assault

In early 1975, the North Vietnamese made a final attack. They quickly swept through many South Vietnamese cities. South Vietnam's president ordered his troops to retreat.

Operation "Frequent Wind"

The day before Saigon fell, the United States sent rescue helicopters into the city. Sixty helicopters flew all day and night to pick up the remaining US citizens and some South Vietnamese. About 8000 people were saved, but thousands more were left behind. In the photograph on the right, people desperately struggle to board a helicopter to escape from the US **embassy** as the North Vietnamese army moved into Saigon.

He needed them to defend the capital of Saigon. Thousands of troops **deserted** instead. More than 500,000 **refugees** moved into Saigon. By the middle of April the North Vietnamese army had surrounded the city.

Saigon falls

On 30 April 1975, North Vietnamese army tanks and trucks rolled into the South Vietnamese capital. The streets were filled with weapons and uniforms left behind by South Vietnamese army troops. Tanks burst through the gates of the presidential palace. The South Vietnamese president quickly surrendered. The Communists renamed the capital Ho Chi Minh City after their heroic leader. After 30 years, the war was finally over.

North Vietnamese troops proudly show their flag after capturing the presidential palace in Saigon.

Entering Saigon

The North Vietnamese met little resistance in the South Vietnamese capital. Colonel Bui Tin remembers:

"That night [April 30], when I sprawled on the lawn of the Independence Palace with members of a communication unit, we all agreed it was the happiest day of our lives because it was a day of complete victory for the nation, because the war ended."

After the war

In October 1978 Chau Van Nguyen, his wife and three young children boarded a small boat in Saigon. The boat was crowded with people all trying to escape from Vietnam. The Nguyens' boat almost turned over during a terrible **hurricane**. A tanker from Taiwan saved them. The family stayed on the boat for twenty days. They were packed into a tight space and did not have much food.

Chau's family was taken to Taiwan. They lived in a camp with other Vietnamese **refugees**. More than a year later, a US church paid for the Nguyen family to go and live in New York state. Many US churches helped Vietnamese refugees with clothes, food, and shelter.

Boat people

The war left much of Vietnam in ruins. As many as three million Vietnamese people may have died. Thousands were left without homes or jobs. People fled from Vietnam on boats, searching for a better life (see photograph below, taken in Saigon in the final days of the war). More than one million "boat people" settled in the United States alone.

Word Bank hurricane severe storm with heavy winds and rain

The United States' pain

People in the United States also suffered after the war. The United States had never lost a war until Vietnam. It was the longest and most costly war the United States had ever fought. Many Americans wanted to forget about Vietnam. To some, this meant forgetting about the men who had fought so bravely. Vietnam **veterans** were not treated as heroes like the soldiers of past wars. Many found it difficult to return to normal life. They could not forget the horror of war. In the years since the war ended, the wounds of the veterans and the nation slowly began to heal. Only in 2000 did the United States finally start trading with Vietnam again.

Fitting tribute

In 1982 the Vietnam Veterans' Memorial opened in Washington DC. The long granite wall lists the names of more than 58,000 US soldiers who died or are still missing in Vietnam. The memorial honours all the American men and women who bravely served during the conflict. It aims to ensure that the soldiers who died in Vietnam will never be forgotten.

TIMELINE

1945
2 September Ho Chi Minh declares Vietnam's independence from France.

1946
December French troops force the Vietminh out of Hanoi.

1954
7 May French surrender at Dien Bien Phu.
21 July Vietnam is officially divided into North Vietnam and South Vietnam.

1960
8 November John F. Kennedy is elected US president.

1963
2 January Viet Cong troops defeat the South Vietnamese army at Ap Bac.
22 November President Kennedy is **assassinated** and Lyndon Johnson takes over as president.

1964
2 August US destroyer USS *Maddox* is attacked by three North Vietnamese **patrol** boats in the Gulf of Tonkin.

1965
2 March Rolling Thunder bombing **campaign** begins.
8 March The first US **combat** troops arrive at Da Nang, South Vietnam.
October – November The Battle of Ia Drang is fought.

1968
21 January The siege of Khe Sanh begins.
30 January The Tet Offensive begins.
24 February The bloody battle for Hue ends.
16 March My Lai **massacre**.

31 March	President Johnson announces he will not run for re-election.
5 November	Richard Nixon is elected president of the United States.

1969
30 April	Number of US troops in Vietnam reaches 543,400.
20 May	The ten-day battle for Hamburger Hill ends.
8 June	Nixon announces the first withdrawals of US troops from Vietnam.
2 September	Ho Chi Minh dies in Hanoi.
15 November	More than 250,000 people take part in a war protest in Washington DC. It is the largest war protest in US history.

1970
4 May	Four students protesting against the war at Kent State University, Ohio, are killed by National Guard troops.

1971
18 August	Australia announces that most of its troops will leave South Vietnam by the end of the year.

1972
18 December	Christmas bombings of Hanoi and Haiphong by the United States begin.

1973
27 January	Peace agreement is signed in Paris, France.
12 February	The first group of US **prisoners of war** is released from North Vietnamese prison camps.
29 March	The last US combat troops leave Vietnam.

1975
30 April	North Vietnamese troops take Saigon.

FIND OUT MORE

Search tips

There are billions of pages on the Internet so it can be difficult to find exactly what you are looking for. These search skills will help you find useful websites more quickly:

- Use simple keywords instead of whole sentences.

- Use two to six keywords in a search, putting the most important words first.

- Be precise – only use names of people, places, or things.

- If you want to find words that go together, put quote marks around them.

Books

American War Library: The Vietnam War – Weapons of War (Lucent Books, 2001)
Examines the guns, aircraft, and other weapons used by US troops in Vietnam.

The Cold War: The Vietnam War, Paul Dowswell (Hodder Wayland, 2002)
A thorough overview of the Vietnam War and its place in the Cold War.

Escape from Saigon: How a Vietnam War Orphan Became an American Boy, Andrea Warren (Farrar/Melanie Kroupa, 2004)
The story of a boy with a Vietnamese mother and an American father who finds a new home in the United States.

Their Names to Live: What the Vietnam Veterans Memorial Means to America, Brent Ashabranner (Twenty-First Century Books, 1998).
Describes the planning and building of the Vietnam Veterans Memorial in Washington, DC. Also includes the life stories of some of the thousands of troops whose names appear on the memorial.

20th Century Perspectives: The Vietnam War, Douglas Willoughby (Heinemann Library, 2001)
Examines how the Vietnam War changed the lives of millions on both sides and helped shape the world in which we live.

Voices from the Past: Vietnam War, Kathlyn and Martin Gay (Twenty-First Century Books, 1996)
A history of the United States' involvement in Vietnam with first-hand accounts from the men and women who served there.

World History Series: The Fall of Vietnam, Philip Gavin (Lucent Books, 2003)
Explains what happened in Vietnam after the Communists took over.

DVD/VHS

Vietnam: A Television History produced by WGBH Boston (1983)
This 13-part series gives a thorough overview of Vietnam's struggle for freedom and how it affected people on both sides of the fighting. Note: the 2004 DVD release includes only 11 parts of the original 13-part series.

Vietnam War with Walter Cronkite (DVD release 2003)
Hosted by Walter Cronkite, the United States' most respected news reporter, this three-part series include a lot of rare interviews and footage from the war that has never been seen before.

These DVDs and VHS contain graphic images of war.

Websites

Most sites are aimed at adults and may contain upsetting information and pictures. Make sure that you use well-known sites with correct information, such as the ones below.

http://www.pbs.org/wgbh/amex/vietnam/
The American Experience: Vietnam Online includes a detailed timeline of the Vietnam War and a Who's Who of all the key leaders.

http://thewall-usa.com/
The Vietnam Veterans' Memorial Wall page is an online tribute to all the US troops who died during the Vietnam War.

www.awm.gov.au/atwar/vietnam.htm
The Australian War Memorial's website includes a full history of Australia's role in the Vietnam War.

www.skp.com.au/memorials/pages/00005.htm
This site gives information on Australia's national monument to Vietnam veterans and casualties.

Disclaimer
All the Internet addresses (URLs) given in this book were valid at the time of going to press. However, due to the dynamic nature of the Internet, some addresses may have changed, or sites may have ceased to exist since publication. While the author, packager, and publishers regret any inconvenience this may cause readers, no responsibility for any such changes can be accepted by either the author, packager, or the publishers.

Where to search

Search engine

A search engine looks through the entire web and lists all sites that match the words in the search box. It can give thousands of links, but the best matches are at the top of the list, on the first page. Try bbc.co.uk/search

Search directory

A search directory is like a library of websites that has been sorted by a person instead of a computer. You can search by keyword or subject and browse through the different sites like you look through books on a library shelf. A good example is yahooligans.com

GLOSSARY

addict person who cannot stop doing something or using something

allies countries that are on the same side during a war

ambush surprise attack

ammunition bullets that are fired from a weapon

artillery large mounted guns that fire shells or missiles

assassinated murdered

battalion large military unit made up of 300 to 1000 troops

booby trap bomb or weapon that is set off when a person touches an object that appears to be harmless

campaign series of related missions that form a phase of a war

ceasefire an end to fighting

civilians people who are not in the armed forces

climate weather conditions for a certain area

Cold War rivalry between the Soviet Union and the United States that began after World War II and lasted until the 1990s

colony country that is ruled by another, more powerful, country

combat fighting

Communist people who support Communism, which is a system of government where all the wealth is shared out equally

comrade fellow soldier

covert secret

demonstrations group protests

deserted left without permission

destroyer fast, lightly armoured but heavily armed warship

detonated exploded

draft order someone into military service

draft cards official letters ordering a person to enter the military

embassy government building of one country that is located in a foreign country

enlightens teaches

evacuate move to safety

grenade weapon that is filled with explosives and can be thrown or launched at a target

guerrilla soldier who is not part of a regular army

gunship helicopter that is armed with several guns or rockets

heroin harmful, illegal drug

horrified shocked

hostile unfriendly

hurricane severe storm with heavy winds and rain

massacre killing a large number of innocent people

Medal of Honour top medal awarded by the US army

MiG jet fighter made by the Soviet Union and flown by North Vietnamese pilots during the war

missing in action (MIA) term used to describe a soldier who does not return from a war alive and whose body is never found

monsoon season period of wind and rain in southern Asia

morale confidence or self-esteem

mortar small, portable cannon

napalm sticky gel made from gasoline that bursts into flames when it hits the air

outraged made very angry

patrol search for enemy troops

platoon small army unit usually made up of 16 to 44 men

prisoner of war soldier who is captured and put in prison by the enemy during the war

protester person who shows that they disagree with, or do not approve of, something

racist someone who hates someone else because of the colour of their skin

rations small amounts of food given to people so they can survive

rebel person who fights against the people who are in power

refugees people forced to leave their home, usually during a war

resolution formal decision that is agreed upon by a vote

rice paddy area where rice is grown

sniper hidden soldier who shoots enemy soldiers from long distances with a special gun

Soviet Union country that once spread aross northern Asia into Eastern Europe and included what is now Russia. Also known as the USSR.

Special Forces top soldiers in the US army

spider hole small one-person hole that is covered with leaves

supply lines means of getting food, medicine, and ammunition

surface-to-air missile (SAM) missile launched from the ground to destroy enemy aircraft

surgery medical operation

tear gas type of gas that makes your eyes fill with tears

torpedo missile that is fired under water

torture beatings and pain inflicted on prisoners, often to get secret information out of them

tour of duty period of time spent in active military service

tripwire wire stretched close to the ground that sets off an explosion when touched

truce agreement to stop fighting

veteran person who served in the armed forces

INDEX

Titles in the *On the Front Line* series include:

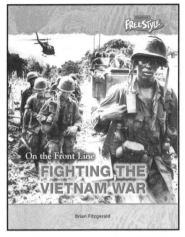

Hardback   1 844 43690 X

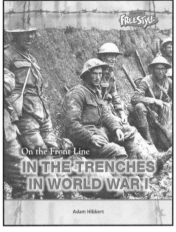

Hardback   1 844 43689 6

Hardback   1 844 43692 6

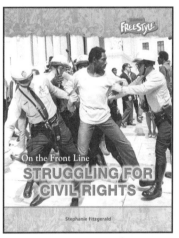

Hardback   1 844 43693 4

Hardback   1 844 43694 2

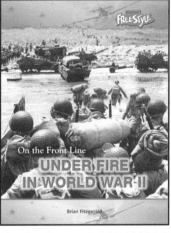

Hardback   1 844 43691 8

Find out about the other titles in this series on our website www.raintreepublishers.co.uk